PROCESS FOR
PURPOSE

inspirational

ANGELA C. GRIFFITHS

1st Printing

PROCESS FOR PURPOSE

ISBN 979-8-332-71050-6

Copyright ©2024 by Angela C. Griffiths

Published by Angela C. Griffiths

DEDICATIONS

I Acknowledged my Lord and Savior Jesus Christ,
who granted me the vision.

I also extend my gratitude to my sister-in-law and brother,
Veronica and Raymond Griffiths.

Additionally, I acknowledge my Pastors, Ricardo McCallum,
and First Lady, Charlotte McCallum. Thank you all for
your support and guidance.

"Process for Purpose is an inspirational book written to encourage and edify you as you pursue your destiny. There are certain processes a person must go through to reach their God-given destiny."

Angela C. Griffiths

TABLE OF CONTENTS

1 PROCESS FOR PURPOSE

When it comes to your purpose, the walk is not easy. It comes with a price. It can become very lonely. It's a lonely walk. When I say lonely, I mean just that—lonely. Throughout this journey, you may find yourself isolated or even abandoned by those who are closest to you, those who say they love you, and those you think would have your back and support you until the end. But instead, some of these people, friends, loved ones, family, and acquaintances will be critical, criticize you, point fingers, and judge you when you are going through hard times.

Some claim they are followers of Christ, forgetting the words of scripture that say, "Those who follow Christ and pursue righteousness will suffer persecution. If we reign with Him, we will suffer as well." This is because you are doing what you are called to do, following what God wants for your life, and living according to His guidance and will.

As you get closer and more focused, you will realize the trials will intensify and become harder to bear. More confusion and unnecessary distractions will arise, and the fire will seem to get hotter. But you must resolve in your heart that, live or die, you will not look or turn back. You must trust Him all the way until you complete your assignment. The obstacles will be great, and the hurdles very high to climb, but if you fail to overcome them, you will have to start over again.

You must be processed in order to walk through your God-given purpose. How can you be a true example or testimony to others unless you have been tried, tested, and gone through your trials and fire? Most people will not listen to you unless you have a personal experience, a living example to say, "I have been there, done that." You can now encourage them, saying, "If I made it, you can as well."

Many times, on this walk, you will get tired. The process is long and tedious. You may decide to give up, but you can't if you are to be influential in people's lives and in the world. You must fight and push forward. Nothing worthwhile comes easy, and without a fight. Remember, the enemy does not fight people who are not going anywhere—only those who are.

Yet Will I Trust Him

The scriptures say, "Even though you slay me, yet will I trust Him." I share this to emphasize that even through tests, there are times in my personal life and walk, including now as I write this book, that I have faced numerous attacks, obstacles, and distractions. Many times, I wanted to give up and quit. But God has been my strong tower, my guiding light, and my strength. When things get rough, I call on Him and cry out to Him to regain my focus and direction. When I think of the many gifts He has given me—gifts that many people lack and are seeking—I realize I cannot be selfish and throw them away. There are people waiting for me to help them move into their purpose and destiny. If I gave up now, I would have failed myself, them, and God. So, I must encourage myself and you to push forward.

God knew you before He created the world. He knew your face, your smile, your heartaches, your pain, and your burdens. He knows when you cry and sees every tear and hears every frustration during times of stress and struggle. He knows the times you would call on Him, the times, places, and reasons for your calls. He knows where you would be even now, at this present time, and what situations and circumstances you would face—family problems, sickness, disease, fears, stressors, financial struggles, torment, oppression, and depression.

Nothing takes the Lord by surprise, and nothing is too hard or too big for Him to stop and conquer. He waits for the opportune time to see how you handle the situations that come your way and if you will try to fight your own battles. Even when you and I fail to handle them properly, He knows. He waits like a gentleman to take over and help us, even when we make mistakes. When we create a mess and fail, He takes the mess and turns it into a message—a message He can use.

He is kind and gentle. He knows our frailties and weaknesses. He doesn't judge us because we fall. Even when we doubt Him, He still gives us what He promised. God has placed within each of us things meant to be released to others. You and I are like rain, meant to pour out onto others to help them grow and find their drive, so they can, in turn, help those God has ordained them to help when it's their turn. It's like a domino effect. So, no matter the fight, the obstacles, the trials, and tribulations—come hell or high water—we are overcomers and victorious, knowing there is nothing too hard for God.

He will continue to fight our battles and remove the obstacles that try to stand in our way. So, continue to fight the good fight of faith, even when it seems like no changes are happening. As you move forward, know that He has your back and is pushing you onward.

Pregnant With Purpose

Are you pregnant with purpose? Unsure if you are and wondering what this really means? Let me explain. When you and I were born, before God predestined and prepared us for the world,

4

He placed gifts within us to bring into the world. Each of us has different gifts from God, not only for ourselves but to help others. Some receive one gift, some two, three, four, or even five. However, the more gifts you have, the more trials, tribulations, and obstacles you will face. You will need to guard and protect these gifts because they are very valuable. These gifts were implanted within you before you were born and they follow you as you grow.

At the opportune time, you need to tap into these gifts and discover what they are. They are often found in your deep passions and desires—things you do well and enjoy without even noticing. These are things you love doing with ease and that come naturally. For some, these activities are done without struggle or difficulty and bring happiness and pleasure, especially when you see the positive results once completed.

While others may struggle, you accomplish these tasks with ease and achieve positive results, known as the aftereffect. Sometimes, you might not be sure what your gifts are and need to pray for the Lord to guide you in discovering and expanding these gifts. It is important not to be fearful but to remain open-minded and willing to explore new areas. Sometimes, we are in the wrong areas and not exposed to the right environments for our gifts to flourish. By being open-minded and trying different things within the ministry, you might find your true calling in an area you never considered before.

Volunteering is another way to expose yourself to new areas you wouldn't normally explore. You never know if you will like something unless you try. This pregnancy with purpose is a burning desire that must come forth. It must be exposed because it is meant to help others who are waiting on you. If it doesn't come forth, you will feel very uncomfortable, discontented, and miserable because you are carrying something that must be shared with others.

This is similar to a natural pregnancy—after nine months of gestation, it's time to deliver the baby. The birthing process takes time and involves pain, pushing, and delivery. Your purpose must be protected by any means necessary.

Giving Birth By Force

Metaphorically speaking, the process of birthing your purpose is similar to the birthing of a baby, and it must be protected by any means necessary, as I stated before. There are haters, vultures, and jealous people who would love to kill and destroy your purpose simply because they don't know their own purpose. They don't want to go through the process of carrying their own purpose; it's too hard. They have made up their minds to stop you before you can give birth to yours because of what you are carrying. It is anointed, powerful, and destined to help others. It will push you to the next level and expose you and your purpose that you have carried through all the hard, fiery trials. Most importantly, it will give God the glory, which many people want for themselves instead of giving God His due.

Even though the process is extremely difficult, you do not look like what you are going through, just like the three Hebrew boys who did not come out smelling like smoke or being burnt despite going through the fiery trials. Due to haters and vultures waiting to execute your purpose during birth, some people have to give birth on the run because they cannot hold it any longer. The pressure becomes fierce, and they have to push and deliver in a safe place by themselves, in isolation.

Some people, in their hurry, step out on their own before God's timing, making a mess of their lives by giving birth prematurely. They were not well-prepared or ready for their purpose, resulting in something half-done that should have been great. Now they must go back to the beginning to develop, mature, and come back fully ready. You cannot rush the process; it takes time.

On the other hand, some people are mature and ready to deliver, but fear, insecurity, lack of support, or financial instability push everything aside. There comes a time in our lives when circumstances force us to walk into our purpose, such as job loss, tiredness, politics, or divorce. These situations push you to do what you are called to do. Once you start, things will eventually fall into place, and you will walk into your purpose.

Sometimes, obstacles and unfair situations try to stop you. You may cry out, "Why me? I did not do anything to deserve this negative situation!" But the Lord says, "Why not you?" As time goes by, you will realize that while it was hard, it was often the enemy causing these negative things to stop and block you from moving ahead. Sometimes it was God's hand, drawing you closer to Him, bringing you to your knees because He sees things in you that need to be worked out. Especially if you are one of His "chosen" vessels, He will not allow you to harm or destroy His people if there are things in you that need to be released before you can work with and around His people.

God has to work on you, putting you on the potter's wheel to work out the kinks and lumps. You will be pulled and stretched to smooth out the rough edges before He releases you to fly like an eagle. This process, while difficult, turns out for your good in the long run. It pushes and forces you into your purpose, allowing you to give birth.

Reflecting back, aren't you happier now than before? Now you can control your own destiny and time. You would never want to return to being mistreated, disrespected, misunderstood, unappreciated, and taken advantage of by organizations and companies that did not appreciate your worth or value.

Now that you know where you are heading and who you are, you understand that the preparation for birthing your purpose takes time. That is why it's called a "process." It does not happen overnight. God has to put some of us to sleep, to do deep surgery on us. Some do not need this, but most of us are hard-headed and stubborn, needing to walk around the wilderness several times instead of just once. Some walked for 40 years and never made it to the promised land to enjoy the Lord's goodness and blessings.

Because of the Lord's grace and mercy, He sometimes puts us to sleep to perform surgery on us. He cuts through layers to chisel away all the deep, dark, and hidden things from our minds and hearts that have hindered, hurt, and tormented us, causing pain for many years. He removes the bitterness, lies, hidden agendas, manipulation, selfishness, self-centeredness, unforgiveness, guilt, shame, and pride. This deep surgery is necessary for us to walk into our purpose and give birth.

God, being a gentleman, does the surgery gently. If He were too harsh, we might revert to our old ways due to the pain. He has to do the surgery slowly and gently to ensure we are ready to take our place and go through the process. This way, we gain the experience needed to be understanding, kind, and able to handle and treat His people with love, as He treats us.

Total submission and surrendering are crucial. Many of us struggle with surrendering, but after repeated surgeries or wandering in the wilderness, we get tired of it. We want to be healed completely, without reopening wounds and starting over again. Yes, it's painful, but it's worth it.

Knowing Your Worth

As you reflect on the many obstacles that have tried to stop and block you from moving forward in the past, remember your value. Remember what you are worth. Your worth is precious and cannot be bought! Many people, whether they are family, friends, or associates, may become jealous of you because you have persevered and left them behind. Because of this, you will be hated and targeted by many. They may smile at you, but deep inside, they harbor resentment. Behind your back, they gossip and slander your name, telling lies to defame you.

Some people won't think you deserve what you have or where you are going, or the place God has elevated you to be. Others wish they were you and want to be you, but they are not willing or able to walk in your shoes and go through what you have endured to be where you are. They have a crab-in-the-bucket mentality; as you climb to the top, they try to pull you down to their level. They don't want to see you progress and become better than they are. Once again, this is a part of your process.

You must remember and remind yourself of the reason why you are doing what you are doing and why you are going in this direction. Remember, the purpose is not about you! It's bigger than you! You are just the vessel being used to fulfill the purpose and give God the glory. Your role is to be an obedient, submissive vessel, helping others that God has placed in your path to care for and guide into their purpose and God-given destiny.

It has nothing to do with you! If it were about you, you would not have chosen this path. As selfish and self-centered as we can be, we would have turned back and done our own thing.

Don't look back! Things will get better, but they will also get harder at times. As you already know, nothing comes easy, especially when you have to work hard for it. Keep moving forward. As you move, God will move and send people to help and guide you. He will certainly send the help you need and give you favor. As many of you already know, those who are entrepreneurs can find mentors and business professionals in your area of expertise to motivate and encourage you through networking events and other resources.

The process you must go through to walk into your purpose and destiny is strenuous and exhausting at times. Some of you will lose everything materially, and some will lose family and friends. Others will turn against you, and you might lose both materially and in terms of relationships. When you are going through this process, most friends won't understand because they cannot grasp what you must endure to get to where God wants you to be. They may not stick around because they can't handle the hardship and cannot support you while you are going through it. Some may call you crazy or lazy just because you are in the midst of your process. Even you yourself may not understand at times what is going on, but you go with the flow because you know the things and circumstances you are facing are not of your own doing.

To be perfected for Kingdom work, one must go through the fire. Trials by fire purify and cleanse, breaking down all that needs purification before the true gold within you shines through. It's not just about looking like gold; the true test comes when you endure the fire.

Maturity does not come with age, or the number of years lived but by how one handles life's trials and tests. It shows in the way you face circumstances and situations. When you are rubbed but not bruised, scratched but not bleeding, dropped but not broken, you know you are fit and ready to go! The enemy will use people, things, and circumstances to break you down so that you give up on purpose, dreams, destiny, or even life itself.

The pressures can and often will get so high and intense that you may feel like death is at your door. You will also be persecuted by those closest to you, including friends, family, associates, and even co-workers. So don't be surprised when you see these things happening. Their demeanor towards you may change; kind words may turn harsh and critical. Lies may be told to get you terminated because of their envy and jealousy. Some want to be you because they see something inside of you that they desire, but they are not bold enough, they are cowards or too lazy to work on themselves. This is why they hate you—because they can't have what you possess, and they are not you.

Tired Of Being Tired

Every day, it's the same routine, day in and day out. When you wake up each morning and dread going to a dead-end job that is going nowhere, or one where you haven't found your niche, it means it's time for a change. How can you live like this, knowing you're just going to a place to pay the bills but feel unfulfilled, unhappy, with no peace, no joy, and no rest? You're just going through the motions.

Try to find that niche, that area that will be fulfilling. If you don't, eventually you will quit. Even if you are making money, it will just be another job. Sometimes, you have to go through various experiences to know what it is you truly want, or else you will end up in the same situation, just paying the bills and going through the motions again. Deep inside, you will be unhappy and dying in spirit. You are not just a job; it's about finding that place where you will eventually have the opportunity to do something meaningful.

When you are tired enough, you will eventually become tired of being tired, tired of being used and abused, tired of not being appreciated for who you are and what you do, tired of being underpaid, overworked, and overlooked, and tired of being stressed out. How long will you give away your value and worth to unappreciative companies and organizations that build their profits and pockets with your efforts? To them, you are just a number. If you keep giving to them, you will eventually die spiritually, and some may even die physically. They will just call the next number in line. It's time to do something about it; it's time to move.

Find time to re-evaluate yourself and the things you know. Don't be afraid. Take it one step at a time and go slowly. Eventually, you will get there. Start with what you do well. Start with what you do best and ask the Lord for guidance. Pray for your understanding to be opened and for wisdom to be given. You have not yet tapped into all your gifts. These are the areas that are hidden and lying dormant within you.

When you said yes to seeking God's will and purpose for your life, many people believed it would be easy. Speaking from my own experience, I did not quite understand the kind and merciful God who paid the price and died for me. Who am I for Him to come down from His throne and sacrifice His loving son, Jesus, for me? All I wanted was to be grateful by seeking and serving Him with all my heart. Who am I? Although it's tough at times, I try to give it my all. Even in my hardest trials, I remember that He is still with me. Even though I can't see Him with my naked eyes, I know He is here fighting all my battles, and in the end, I win.

I am encouraging you and letting you know that things do not get easier just because you say yes. But it gets easier to let go and let Him handle the hard things you cannot control. In my personal observation, it seems to get harder the higher you elevate. The process is intense! He is processing you into your purpose. Sometimes, the Lord allows the enemy to test you, to see what you are made of, to see if you will give up easily.

Many times, out of frustration, we want to give up because our flesh is tired. The enemy is fighting hard to win you over. The enemy does not fight people who are going nowhere; he fights those who are going somewhere, and that somewhere is not within him.

Surprise! Just in case you did not already know this, it will be no surprise when it comes. You will be prepared. As you elevate and progress, know this: some, or most, of your present friends and close family members will not understand the changes you are or will go through and the decisions you will have to make.

Through your struggles and times of difficulty, many will fall away. They will disappear, and it is at this time you will know who your true friends and family are. You will get no support. Most of them will disappear, and even some of your significant others, including spouses, will be gone as well. Once again, when your purpose is being fulfilled, those who are not predestined to come alongside you will disappear. They cannot go with you. If they try, they will only hinder you and pull you backwards. They will be a stumbling block in your way.

Most will hurt you, discombobulate you, and make you lose focus. You believe that because they are family, they wouldn't do wicked and evil things to you. Get over it! It is what it is! This too shall pass. It's just a distraction to keep you from moving forward and completing your assignment. Yes, it hurts. The ones closest to you will hurt you the most. They cannot sit at the table with you. They cannot go where you are going! All they can do is observe from a distance. And when you get there, they will know it's God's hand on your life.

Jealousy And Critical People

When you reach your destination, you will encounter haters. Another surprise awaits: when you get there, the true secret haters will appear, all of them. Some so-called friends and associates, and even some so-called brothers and sisters within the body of Christ, spouses, families, strangers, and acquaintances, will reveal their true colors. They don't know what you have been through but lift your head up and stand tall. Let their jealousy burn because they cannot stop you. They don't think you deserve it because they were not there during your struggles, so they believe you don't deserve your success. They want to be you.

They want to have what you have. They want the blessings without the tests, trials, and processing. They only want the blessings, not the Blesser. They left you when you needed them the most during your deepest struggles and fears. Regardless of whether they are your best friends, family, or acquaintances, they are not meant to be by your side. God will move them away from you, even in times of difficulty. The Lord always has the right people hidden and ready to help you at the right time.

These people are known as the "ram in the bush" and "destiny helpers." God doesn't let them come out until the appointed time, when He sees you are ready, according to His timeline. The process for purpose, this walk, is a lonely one. Most of the time, it's desolate and you will feel isolated because God has to separate you in order to talk with you. You need to focus completely to hear what He is saying and follow His instructions for the next step or level.

Sometimes, you will not hear Him at all! He gets quiet and stays silent. An acquaintance once said to me, while I was going through some struggles, that while you are taking the test, God remains silent. He is silent, no matter how many questions you ask, because it's a test! The teacher doesn't talk while you are taking a test. It was very clear to me after she spoke those words. I understood what she meant; it's like sitting in a classroom taking an exam. You cannot ask the teacher for any explanations or clarifications, as that would be cheating. At the right time, God will connect you with the right people, called "purpose connections" and "destiny helpers."

During my quiet time, I sometimes read books on business. As you and I venture out into life and business, one must have two or three selected people in their life called mentors. These people go beyond friendship. They are not just associates; they will love and guide you despite your faults. They will tell you things you don't want to hear, even if you don't like it. They are in your life to help mold and support you into the best person God wants you to be. They will be there through thick and thin, through your ups and downs, the good and the bad. These people are authentic and real, and they are rarely found. You must pray for the Lord to send them. These are the two or three people you need in your close, intimate circle.

As you move forward, you will meet many people, but you must pray for God to reveal who the genuine ones are. Many people will be obstacles as you move ahead. Most will want to be close to you because of who you are and where you are going, where the Lord is taking you. They want to hitch a ride, piggyback on your success. They will do just about anything to be close to you. Some will even try to buy your friendship. Be cautious.

Your looks, character, and personality will attract both love and hate. Some people who don't know you will love you, and most will hate you because of these three things. When you are hated, it's usually because others see something in you, they want or want to be. Simply put, they want what you have. They desire the qualities in you. They may not be friendly, but you are, and they are jealous. They may not be approachable, but you are. They are not real, authentic, or genuine. When they smile, it's fake, but when you do, it's genuine. You're honest and straightforward, while they are snakes, backstabbers, and liars who hate themselves for being that way.

In you, they see what they could look like and what they could be. So, in turn, you are hated. But continue to be the person God intended for you to be. Don't change a thing and strive to improve even more. Don't change unless the Lord says so. Let them be convicted by your lifestyle.

2 THE DAILY FIGHT AND STRUGGLES

As we go through our daily lives, unexpected challenges will arise. While we are minding our own business, things happen beyond our control. People influenced by the enemy will try to block and stop our progress. Regardless of what comes our way, we must stay focused and trust God. Nothing takes God by surprise. Trust in His word and in His promises. Whether the struggles are in your family relationships, job, business, marriage, health, or finances. These are four common areas the enemy attacks. He aims to get you off track, causing you to worry and lose your faith, trust, and hope in God. But know this: regardless of what is going on in your life, if you have no power to fix it, you must leave it in God's hands. Lay it at His feet and trust Him to fix it.

I know the resistance and struggles can be overwhelming. The urge to try and constantly fix things is strong. One moment, you lay it down at His feet in total surrender, and the next, when it seems to be taking too long, you pick it up again, trying to fix it yourself. But there comes a time when we cannot fix things on our own because they are beyond our control. God sets it up this way so you will get frustrated and have no choice but to leave it in His hands. He wants you to trust Him completely, so you won't pat yourself on the back. He wants to get all the glory and accolades when He brings you through, and the haters will know without a doubt that it's God who brought you through.

Before it all ends, some of you will suffer great ordeals and make great sacrifices because you said yes. This is part of the process and the God-given purpose for where you are heading in your life. This is the path the Lord has you on, and you cannot detour until the assignment is completed. The hands of God are on your life, so be still, stay focused, and set your sights on your calling. Despite the distractions, focus on what you are supposed to do.

Some of you are already marked by the enemy for assassination, but he cannot and will not allow the enemy to take you out. Your Creator's hands are on you, ordering your footsteps. Even when you think you messed up, the Lord knew you would! He kept you, turning your mishaps into something beautiful. The scripture says, "What the devil meant for evil, God turns it around for your good."

You should have been dead already, but because of His grace and mercy, you are kept. You should have overdosed on drugs, but He kept you! You have purpose; you must fulfill this call to help pull out the many. Why you? Because you are special in His eyes, and that's why you are targeted for assassination by the enemy. You are chosen, the apple of His eye, gifted, strong, and courageous. You are a gift from God to the world, handpicked by the Almighty for such a time as this. Selected to help guide lost souls, crying out for deliverance and freedom from the tormentor.

As the end draws near, you are selected to go out and win them before it's too late. Some of you should have been in an asylum, depression took over, but it could not take you out. The stage of suicide— the devil says yes, but the Holy Spirit says no. No, I need you here to fulfill your purpose during your lifetime here on earth. No, not yet, says the Lord, and not this way.

Many have suffered by the hands of people used by the enemy to oppress you—physical, emotional, and psychological stressors used against you to take you out. Once again, your Father says no. Not so. He has chosen you for such a time as this, to be strong and to go through the pain. But He is with you all the way. You are never alone, even if it feels that way at times. No, my child, I will never leave nor forsake you, even unto the end of days. I will be with you, I will be at your side, I will guide you. Listen, and you will hear my voice. Listen, and you will recognize and know my voice. It is me, not you. I will continue to pour my spirit within you, so you will be more like me. The world will know for sure it's me in you.

Pushed out, like a young eaglet pushed out of its nest by the mother, you will face the world, but not without the protection of guardian angels in the unseen realm, following you daily. No matter where you go or what situation you may find yourself in, nothing takes Daddy God by surprise. It may surprise you, but it's no surprise to Him. Nothing that happens to you is a mistake; it's a setup to make you stronger.

Some have lost jobs, businesses, homes, and health. But regardless of what or how much you have lost, there is still hope. It's painful losing things you have worked hard for, things you put time and effort into accomplishing. The tears behind the loss are real, but although it's hard and difficult, there is still hope because you are alive. In time, you will regain what you have lost, even better than before. Despite the loss of income from jobs and businesses, some of you became homeless and had to seek shelter, sleep in your cars, but that was your shelter. The good Lord never left you; He was with you through your ordeal. He kept you in your right mind!

He kept you focused so you could think about your next move, your next strategy. While you were silent and worried, He was talking and setting up things for your progress and advancement. While you were depressed and worried about how things would work out, God had already worked it out. He had to hide some of you in the background so they wouldn't have their mouths on you.

He had to develop and refine your character for the major exposure when the time came to take you from the background to the forefront.

He had to hide some of you on the backside of the desert so He could pour into you, preparing you like John the Baptist preparing the way for Jesus. This was done so you can be prepared, so the light in you can shine in dark places. You will be one of the ones to pluck up, pull down, root up, and plant. Before all of this is done, you will know for sure this is God's doing, and He will get all the glory.

There will come a time in your life very soon when you will experience total freedom because you have forgiven and let go of the things and people of the past and present that used and abused you. You have also forgiven yourself for the foolish and stupid mistakes you made over and over again. You have passed the test! You have made it through the trials that tried to keep you down because you have finally recognized that it was only a test, and this too shall pass. The pain you felt, you won't feel again. This is when peace comes. No one can bind you anymore. Before, you allowed it. Now, you will have your rest! Now the joy comes after the weeping.

Most of all, the Lord God is pleased with you! You have fought a hard battle, a good fight for a good cause, and now He is pleased with you. Now you will enter into that resting place. The battle is not over, but the Lord will cause even your foes and enemies to be at peace with you. All the words spoken over your life will now come to pass, and the material things will follow.

The enemy won't be able to touch you because this is your season of rest to enjoy the blessings that have been held up for so long. The Lord won't allow the enemy to disturb your peace because you have earned it. The enemy can do nothing, no matter who they are. Just sit back and observe. Some of them will die while they look on what God has done in your life, because they must swallow their words and the evil they tried to put on your life. Now they must suffer the consequences of what they said that did not come to pass in your life.

They did not fulfill the works of the devil towards you, so now they must pay the consequences. It's a deal and sacrifice they made with Satan himself to take you out. Because you did not die as they wanted, the sacrifice must be repaid to the devil—their life and family for yours. People do not realize that the scripture says, "Touch not my anointed, and do my prophets no harm." This simply means when a person sows a bad seed, they are going to reap a bad harvest. They will reap what they sowed towards you. They must pay the devil back for the sacrifices of their soul and blood covenant.

Just imagine when a seed is planted in the ground. It's just one seed! But when the tree from that seed grows and starts to bear its fruit, it produces many fruits from that one seed. So now, what was planted will be reaped. There is no turning back. It's already in the ground. While the tree was young, there were many chances to pull it up and destroy it. But instead, they kept watering and fertilizing it until it started to bear fruit. Now it's too late. The person who planted the seed will reap the fruits from that tree.

All the breakthroughs promised by the Lord will now arrive. The finances you have been waiting for, the business, the ministry, the children, and family set free, saved, and delivered. The sickness and diseases healed. Addicts are no longer addicted. The right spouse arrived, and marriage took place. The relationships in the family improving, the turmoil resolved. Things you lost restored. Breakthrough upon breakthrough!

Supernatural miracles happening! Now you are truly the head and not the tail. The hardship you once suffered is only a memory. Victory after victory in almost everything. Those who are in prison were released and set free. The barren woman now able to give birth. Favor after favor. Experiencing the favor of God's greatness through strangers set up in your path. Even some who were dead are now alive—God raised up.

Experiencing The Freedom in Your Purpose

The process for purpose was set up from the beginning because now you are walking totally in your purpose, a miracle worker for God, used and approved by God himself. You are experiencing the freedom in your purpose, and now you can walk totally free. The people you are supposed to connect with at this time will find you, and you will find them.

The work you are purposed to do will be easy; all that you need to do will flow easily. As you accomplish them, it may not come easy, but it will flow easily. All whom the Lord sends your way will be definitely connected to you, and you will experience God's glory from you to them. A total fulfillment, total peace, and rest in Him. Once again, you cannot have a testimony without going through the test.

As you look back on all you have been through in your past, it will be a thing of the past. Your future will be bright and beautiful. Then you will ask yourself, "Was it worth it?" Only you can answer that question. Would you want to go through what you have been through to be where you are now? Only you can answer these questions.

Experiencing the freedom and fulfillment God has purposed for you because you said yes! Yes, to the call, yes to His will, and obedience, no matter the cost! Yes, for you I will live, and for you I will die. Otherwise, life won't be worth living.

Surrendered by His love, glory, and kindness, knowing who He is, is knowing His heart desires. Everyone who is called must be processed and go through the process to pass the test to reach that God-given destination. If you fail the tests, you must take them over and over again. And when you are taking these tests, the teacher is always silent to see if you have retained and learned from the examples that were given to you, life experiences.

The tests are critical to pass because they are lives and souls that are at stake that will be entrusted to you. Tests of pain, stress, trust, patience, faith, confidence, hope, love, caring, tenderness, kindness, among the fruits of the spirit found in Galatians chapter 5: joy, peace, patience, love, kindness, goodness, gentleness, and self-control. Long-suffering. He must be able to trust you with whatever responsibilities He is rendering in your hands.

You must go through in order not to cause a shipwreck. You must go through in order for no premature delivery. Premature delivery can cause death of your purpose and destiny and also shame and embarrassment to you and the work of God. That's why the completion of the process is necessary. It's a must to fulfill the call.

The process comes when you are going through it! You can pray to get out of it, but you must go through. And no one else can go through it for you. If you are to succeed in your purpose, crying, screaming, or fasting won't do it either. Getting help from others may only help to a certain point, but only the Lord can truly help and guide you through. We are only instruments or vessels surrendered to be used for His purpose.

Testimony

When I surrendered over 20 years ago, I did not know I was being processed for purpose. At the beginning, I told the Lord whatever He wanted me to do, I would do, and to use me however He chooses to use me. Once again, the flesh wanted me to fight and forfeit the promise I made to the Lord. Yes, it's true. Many obstacles and fights from the enemy arose to stop my purpose. Many times, I wanted to give up and give in because the fire was turned up very high, and the distractions were intense. I could not focus many times; I put the books away and stopped writing for years at a time because other priorities were at hand, and the enemy used this to disrupt my focus. Most of it was either problems with losing my job or not making enough, or my relationship problems with my marriages, and the family problems. I cried many times to the Lord and asked, what does He expect of me when I have no job to pay my bills, get evicted and homeless? How can I focus on my writing? I wanted to give up! Many times, I said to myself, if I had known I would be going through all of this, I would not have accepted the assignment. But I did, and regardless of the obstacles in my life, I continued to try, and God always worked it out.

When the storm comes, it reveals who we truly are! When you are destined for purpose, all hell will break loose in your life. The spiritual forces of darkness will try to stop you intentionally. It's not about how you start, but when you finish. The enemy is worried about where you are going.

3 USE YOUR PAIN TO BIRTH YOUR DESTINY

This message speaks not only to me but also to you! Use your pain, suffering, and trials to propel you to your purpose and destiny. Utilize the deepest hurt to launch you into what you didn't know was within you. Employ the sexual abuses, physical, emotional, and mental abuse you endured. Utilize seclusion, loneliness, and isolation. Channel the pain of divorce, loss of loved ones through death, abuse, and injustice. Harness the heartbreak of betrayal and teasing. Leverage the pain of unfair treatment on jobs or prejudice due to your color or nationality. Draw strength from the pain of judgment for doing what's right. Utilize the anger to propel you forward. Utilize the pain of tortures, verbal abuses, and rejection, along with other suffering you've endured—those you can't bring yourself to mention to anyone else. The only utterance is from your mouth to God's ears, from your thoughts to His ears. Utilize the pain; it serves a purpose. It provokes you to the next level, helps others who can't speak for themselves or help themselves, aids those going through what you've already experienced. It helps you help them to birth and guide them through their pain into the fullness of their destiny. Moreover, it helps those you least expect. You are helping birth their purpose in their lives.

The anointing you carry is born from tough pain, suffering, and struggles in your life. To birth ministry, business, and to have a testimony, one must go through the testing of fire. A person of wisdom won't listen; they want to hear the end results of how you did it and made it through. People want to hear reality, not just talk with no experiences or action to back it up. All that you and I have been through—sometimes we think it's a waste of time, idle time, and time lost. But I realize it's not wasted at all! There is a season for everything, a process of time, lessons learned. In these times of hard times, frustration, suffering, trials, and pain, God is working on and in us, developing us into who He truly wants us to be.

In these times, He is also removing obstacles, tearing down roadblocks that the enemy is setting or has set to derail our path to our destiny. So, in times of trials, pain will be used as fuel to empower us into birthing. All the things you have gone through are not wasted; they're past and present experiences push you to better serve, to get to the place of purpose. Prophetic words spoken over our lives in the past—some many years ago—may seem forgotten by God, but He hasn't forgotten. It's not that they will not come to pass;

it's just that we often expect them to manifest immediately. Some words require life experiences before they come to fruition. If we do not learn and experience certain things and change our mindset, we won't know how to handle them when they come. So, we must wait to be equipped to handle what God has gifted us with.

Example Joseph and His Brothers

A perfect example is from the Book of Genesis. Chapter 37 39-40. This is talking about Joseph. Who suffered. From the hands of his own brothers. As a slave from age 17- 30 years old. This was a total of 13 years he suffered. Because of hated and jealousy, because of his gift! The suffering came from his own Family. Who first conspired against him to murder him. But because this wasn't in God's plan for his purpose and destiny. He allowed them. To put him in a pit. and sold as a slave. He was brought down into Egypt and was sold again to man called Potiphar. He was captain of the guards. For King pharaoh. He was placed in this man's house to oversee Everything. And his wife wanted to fornicate. With him every day she. Try to entice and tease him to have sex with her. And when he would not, she lied to him. To her husband. Who was very angry and locked him up in jail Now, while he was in the jail God gave him favor. And he was overseeing the prisoners at this time in the jail. During this time, he met. King's Pharaoh Butler. And his Baker. And both men had dreams. And Joseph was able to interpret these dreams to these men, and they came to pass. One was killed. And one went back to his job. Serving the king. Of course, at this time, the one that lived and went back to serve the King promised that. When he gets back with in the good graces of his boss the king he would speak. On his behalf! Unfortunately, some people sometimes. Once people get want, they want they forget their promises. And this was one of those times. So Two years later The king Pharaoh had a dream. And no one could interpret this dream. And. At this time. The Butler remembered his promise. That Joseph was the only one there that Could it interpret these dreams and it was this time that Joseph was called and brought up. To the king. To interpret. These dreams. So, to make a long story short. Because of the interpretation, and wisdom that he had, God gave him favor with men. He was favored by God. And now Joseph became Governor of Egypt, second in charge to King, pharaoh. So eventually. If you read the story. You will see. Eventually, those same brothers. Had to come to joseph for food to save their lives. From the same dreams that they hated him for.

So, I mentioned this story. To say this. You will suffer and go through many things by the hands men, you may or may not know. But throughout all the struggles, the suffering. When you go through. It's all. A process. To get you to your destination. Where God wants you to be, it doesn't matter how long! You will get there at the appointed time.

The Birthing Experience Should Make Us Mature

As we face life's challenges, we should mature and become better equipped to handle life's difficulties, especially if we evaluate ourselves, recognizing where we have been and where we are going. This self-awareness helps us manage situations and frustrations better. We learn to avoid unnecessary battles, leaving them in God's hands, and walking away from foolish fights that the enemy uses to engage us. Recognizing these distractions allows us to focus on battles meant for God. Tell the devil to get behind you and go back to the pits of hell from where he came.

Words Of wisdom

A preacher once told me that dirt is part of your process. He said people will be used by the enemy to throw dirt on you when they think there is no hope left for you, or when they believe you are done, washed up, or worth nothing. But you are something. God is using the foolish things in your life—the good, the bad, and the ugly—to elevate you to the next level.

Those who throw dirt on you, thinking they have buried you, will see and wonder what has happened to you. They will know it was God all along, and He will get the glory. So, I say to those who love to throw dirt and bury others, be careful. The ones you bury may just be the ones God will use to help pull you out of your grave. Be careful of the stones you throw! Be mindful of the words you speak when others are going through trials.

Don't be too quick to judge someone who is suffering trials and having a hard time. Don't assume they are suffering because of something they did wrong or because of the life they are living. Some religious people love to criticize and judge others, forgetting where the Lord brought them from. Have you ever considered that they might be going through trials because they are doing the right thing? The enemy is not happy to see someone trying to serve God and live an upstanding life.

Remember, nobody is perfect, but striving to live righteously in the sight of God is part of the journey. Use the pain and challenges to push yourself closer to God and grow in your faith.

At times, you may feel on the brink of giving up because it's too hard. Everywhere you look, there are trials. Every time you try, it ends in disappointment, failure, hurt, and pain. The enemy whispers to you, "Why keep trying? Nothing is working. Everything you put your hands to fails. Where is the God you serve? You may as well give up! What sense does it make to try so hard when you keep failing? It doesn't make sense. Give up and give in." Fight like a good soldier. Come on, fight the good fight of faith. God has not brought you this far to leave you now! He has Your back.

Even when the enemy uses other people to harm you, to do evil toward you, or to push you out of character and into doing something insane, don't do it. He is only trying to set you up to humiliate you and laugh at you when you mess up and go beyond the point of no return. Don't kill yourself, even as he whispers lies in your ears that this will resolve your problems. Don't get yourself in trouble with the law because of evil people.

Don't listen to his lies telling you it will be better. Don't believe the lies urging you to return to the world, or to accept an offer to convert to him, promising that everything will improve. He will whisper these lies in your ears, claiming your struggles will be over and that he will give you everything to make you happy. Lies! Don't fall into that trap. Don't fall for it. This is also a part of your pain to make you strong, to endure, to trust God, and to keep the faith.

The Year 2020

The year 2020 has tested and tried many people. Faith has changed lives, and many have been tried by fire; this is how many people's lives and existence have been. It was one of the toughest times ever. Some have questioned their faith and wondered if there is a God allowing all this to happen. Some have fallen off, collapsed, and gone back into the world. Many of the churches in the body of Christ have failed and are falling apart as the world and country have separated. This is also a part of the birth pains. We cannot just live flaky, materialistic lives.

When hard times come, we fall apart. It's more than that. We must be sustained by His eternal Spirit that will keep us no matter what comes our way. An unshakeable strength of hope, faith, confidence, love, and trust, knowing that He will keep us no matter what comes or goes, no matter if we are in good or bad times.

Sometimes God isolates us for pruning, years of preparation for excellence. But first, the isolation is to see what comes out of us when we are in a trial or trying times. He wants to see, when the refining hour comes, what we are made of! When the trials of life come, if there are any motives within us, if we come only to get from Him, or if we will remain even more faithful. When the fire of life comes knocking at our door, will we still love Him? Will we still serve Him and do what He asks us to do? Or will we leave and move on to whatever we think can suffice our needs? The hurts and life's fiery darts—will they cause us to dry up and fall away like a leaf in the fall season?

But I can also say that 2020 allowed many people to explore and evaluate their lives and find out what they were made of. Some found their true purpose and destiny and left their nine-to-five jobs and started their own businesses. Part of the process is character building. God has to see what you are made of! We have flaws such as insecurities, anger issues, and some are gossipers, inquisitive, or in other words, nosy. So that is one purpose for character building.

We are under construction. When people come against us, sometimes it is in God's plan to see how we are going to react! He is building maturity. We have to trust Him when things don't make sense or go our way. The mistakes we make will not stop God's plans for our lives. The Book of Jeremiah Chapter 29 verse 11 says, "For I know the plans I have for you, declares the Lord, plans to prosper you and not to harm you, plans to give you hope and a future."

So, no matter what it looks like or what it feels like in your present situation, or what it feels like, although it seems impossible and doesn't make sense, even when you are doubting! He still has you covered, still has your back. Even though you are stressed and fearful, He still has your back! He is building your faith, confidence, and hope, including trust. Trusting in Him even in and through this! Stressing or being upset? Is not and will not resolve the problems. It just exacerbates it and makes it worse. Even doing it afraid take faith. As you walk and trust Him day by day. Until the change comes. Remove yourself and focus on some positive relaxation techniques. Do things you like that will distract you from negative thoughts. Think, listen, and breathe. Breathing techniques, love relaxation will help to calm your spirit. Inhalation, inhale, and exhale through your nostrils. Hold your breath for three to four seconds and then slowly exhale through your mouth. Repeat a few times.

A person cannot concentrate on two things at the same time. One has to stay focused to remove the other. Another example is listening to positive, upbeat music or teachings, and thinking about positive words. Meditation, soothing waves of the ocean, or raindrops.

Exercise, such as walking or jogging, observation, and looking at the beauty of nature, such as going to the beach or lakes, observing the trees, and hearing the birds, a field of flowers, will help to distract your thoughts. Spend time reading, and if you enjoy fishing, this will help ease and relax your stressful mind. A person can use any of these techniques to help relax and calm.

The emotions and spirit, but with all this, it does not take the place of the Lord and the peace that He gives. It's times like this people should draw closer to God, but instead, they run further away from Him and make things worse by trying to define other things to replace or substitute Him because of anger and fear. At times like this, talking releases what's on your mind. Talking with someone you trust, with family members that are positive, friends. This is not a time to isolate yourself. If you do, you will fall into stages of depression, even though this is still a part of the process.

Although things are difficult at this present stage of your life, if you keep the faith and keep holding on to God, even when it does not look like there is anything changing, you must continue to trust Him! Not men, not the government, not your friends or family, not even the President. They are not your source. But God! Not even the things He blesses you with but focus on Him. And He will use people to be a blessing to you. But do not focus on the people. Be thankful, but they are not your God.

He will bless you with stuff, but don't focus on these things. You were blessed with them. You are blessed to have them. But the things are not God. Again, focus on Him. There are more people and things He will use to bless you, only if you stay focused on the Blesser.

Some people have stuff, but the stop cannot bring or give them peace. It's a temporary fix. It cannot give them joy. Once that wears off, there is nothing else to hold onto. More stuff brings temporary joy, but true joy and peace come from God. At times, even when we know Him, we tend to take our eyes off Him, and the discontentment we feel when we do that is very painful. It makes us wonder about those who don't know Him at all, how they live day by day without a Savior. Once again, it does not matter what it looks like, He will make a way for you, or His, and He will take care of His own! That's a promise, you will not die.

Many people in this time and season are blessed and prospering. So why do you think He is going to bless and prosper them and let you suffer? He is not a respecter of people. He said it in His Word. It may not be your time yet! But hold on, it is coming. Don't be jealous of anyone. Don't block your blessings. Your time is coming. Your life is a testimony that God will use to deliver many. That is the reason I see your time is coming for your blessing. The reason is because the Lord is continually pruning you. He is continually chipping away the dead things to make you grow, to perfect you, and to make you more like Him. People are watching your life. You will never be completely perfect, but perfect enough in His eyes. When He chooses to release you into your season of blessings, then the world will know it was not you who caused the blessing, it was Him.

The people will know and be drawn to Him, not you. He will draw them, and they will want what you have. The world loves material things, so they will be drawn to these at first. Then they will realize it's more than that. It's because of the God in you they seek after. Because material things alone won't bring peace.

4 GOD'S GRACE

God's grace is the free and unmerited favor of God. Grace is the power that God willingly gives us to help us do what we could never do on our own. God does not give any assignment without His grace. Grace no longer relies on human strength and capacity. It's God carrying you and I. He works through us. The grace He gives us makes whatever we need to do stress-free. He gives us the help we need through His grace to perform the work or chores needed to be done. Without His grace, we would not be able to do the assignment; we would not be able to do what we do. We cannot take any credit in any way. Yes, you surrendered yourself to be used freely. It's called free will. But you can't do the work without His power, and He willingly gives us help. Second Corinthians Chapter 12, Verse 9, and 1st Corinthians 15, Verse 10, talk about these things, about His grace and power. So, it is God who gives us the grace to do what we do.

Don't take credit for whatever you accomplish. It is God who gives you the power and drive to do all things creatively.

Your tomorrow is greater than your past. It is greater than what you have been through. The anointing comes from breaking, beating, that we had to experience something in order to have a testimony to tell others and to encourage them so they can come through their test. Anointing costs. It costs great sacrifices and tests.

In order to give birth to something, a person must go through something. They must go through the labor, stretching, tugging, and pulling. Labor is hard work. Labor is pain. Then comes the delivery, leading to birth. So, the process involves great struggles.

Experiences of Life, Life's Nugget's

The experiences that a person gains cannot be bought with money. In other words, money can't buy the life experiences that shape a person as they journey through life, and these experiences cannot be taught by anyone, including professors or teachers. These are essential experiences that help individuals grow and develop, both for themselves and for others.

Being the black sheep of your family can be challenging. Are you feeling disliked by your family, friends turned foes, associates, co-workers, bosses, or ex-spouses? One thing you need to realize is this, you didn't choose your family. The Lord placed you in it. While you can distance yourself, you can't erase them. However, you can remove so-called friends, associates, bosses, and co-workers from your life whom you'll never have to see again.

As we navigate life's experiences, sometimes God sends enemies our way, known as God-sent enemies, to elevate us to the next level of our life's calling. It may not feel good at the time because they challenge us, pushing us to our limits and revealing aspects of ourselves that need improvement. They are akin to a "thorn in the flesh." Yet, they serve a purpose, pushing us to grow and develop.

God also uses circumstances as irritants to push us along the path, teaching us to trust and depend on Him completely rather than on other people. When our minds are at peace, we are in a position of power. In this state, we are not distracted, frustrated, stressed, or disturbed. It is then that we can clearly see our enemies, as God fights our battles while we rely solely on Him.

Your Enemies

Stay humble in your integrity! Treat others the way you would want to be treated. This can be challenging at times because people may not treat you the way you treat them, for various reasons. If they don't treat you well, remember this, they have to answer to God for their actions. While it may not feel good, you don't need to worry about answering to God for how you respond to them. If you don't react to their mistreatment, you're doing the right thing. I can personally attest to this. It's not easy. Sometimes, our natural inclination is to fight back, but by God's grace, we can remember to do what is right by asking ourselves, "Would He be pleased with what I am doing?"

It's important to remember that we are ultimately accountable to God, not to other people. So, even when you are kind to those who mistreat you, even when they mock you or speak ill of you, continue to do what is right, and let God handle them through conviction.

Stand firm in your integrity. In the end, they will be the ones who look foolish, and their lives will eventually start to unravel. As Proverbs 16:18 says, humility comes before honor, so don't take credit when you see the Lord moving and your prayers being answered as you trust Him to fight your battles.

As you witness the downfall of your enemies who try to oppose you, remember to stay true to your integrity and let God be the one to bring justice.

5 CARRYING YOUR CROSS

Part of the process involves bearing and carrying your cross. Luke 9:23 says, "Whoever wants to be my disciple must deny themselves and take up their cross and follow me." So, if you want to follow Jesus, you must bear your own cross. This means you will face trials similar to being in Egypt, in bondage, or in the valley. You might encounter your own Red Sea, fiery furnace, lion's den, or deep waters. But even when you feel like you're in deep waters, He will not let you drown.

He will not allow the fiery flames to burn you because you must fulfill the destiny and purpose for your life. You must accomplish the reason you were born, the reason you were created on earth. You must fulfill your calling before God calls you home. Sorrows, pain, persecution, tribulations, and hurt will come.

The raging storm will come with anger, stress, frustrations, bitterness, oppositions, sadness, and at times, depression. These may be followed by isolation, loneliness, and feelings of abandonment and desertion. Everyone has their seasons of going through fiery furnaces and deep waters. This is part of life's journey, but we don't stay there. Each day brings something new; no days are identical.

You may ask, how can anyone make it through this journey when life is so hard? This is why we know we cannot make this journey on our own. Sometimes we feel alone, but we are not. We must hold on to the unchanging hands of God, or else we will all die in vain and face premature death. This is what the enemy is waiting for.

This is why, as people, whether unsaved or saved like me, we sometimes feel lonely. As a single woman, I experience loneliness because God made humans to have a helpmate to complement each other. However, God created each of us to commune with Him. Mere human companionship cannot complete us; only God can.

That is why nothing can fill that void, no money, no sex, no drugs, no alcohol, and no material things. This is one of the reasons some people, even with all the money in the world, commit suicide. They kill themselves because there's a void that needs filling, and money and material things cannot fill that deep hole.

It's good to have money! But don't let money be your god. It can't buy true love, healing, real friendship, take away pain, or fill the void in our hearts. It can't give true peace of mind.

In this season of my life in 2021, I experienced great suffering, immense pain, and hurt. I endured major betrayal of my love and trust, disrespect, hatred, and being despised by my own family, my daughter, aunt, and niece, for doing good for them. I gave up my life, my job, my apartment, and relocated to help save their lives. In return, they called the police on me to put me out on the street, took me to court, and evicted me without compensation for my time. It was an extremely painful ordeal. Talk about carrying your cross! This is the reality of being stabbed in the back and betrayed, like Judas did to Jesus, by your own family.

Sometimes, during our season of suffering, we cry out to God for it to be over. But it seems to carry on endlessly, as though there is no end in sight. We can't always cry away at what is not completed. It appears God allows a period of time to go by, and you and I must pass the test in order to move on. Instead of crying it away, we must ask the Lord to carry us through and help us build faith, trust, and confidence in Him. When other difficult times come, we will remember our past and how He carried us through. It was not by our own strength, but by His, so His name will be glorified.

I also remember another horrible season in my life. In 2019, I made the wrong choice by marrying an abuser. I suffered major losses and almost lost my life. I called the police after he harassed me by phone at my job. He almost paralyzed me due to physical abuse to my neck and back on my birthday because I went out by myself, came home, and kissed him goodnight. I endured mental and emotional abuse at the hands of my ex-husband.

I spent 14 days in jail for kissing him, which was considered assault because he did not want to be touched. I went to court, and the case was thrown out. While I was in jail, I lost my job. My daughter was ashamed of me, lied about trying to get me released, and was very short with me when talking. She believed my ex-husband instead of me. I was locked out of the house by him, had all my personal belongings thrown away, and ended up in a battered women's shelter.

Despite all the pain I went through, God saw me through. What you are experiencing now or in the future are experiences gained for the processing of your purpose, just like me! God will carry and see you through as well. No matter where you find yourself—in the valley, the fire, or on top of the mountain—the Lord God is no respecter of persons. He will see you through. He promised He will never leave nor forsake you and me, even when we don't deserve it. Because of His loving kindness, grace, and mercy, He will continue to love, protect, and keep us.

He will lead you to and through until you reach your destined purpose. It may be slow and tedious, but you will get there. Frustrations will come, but they are working patience in you. Patience and long-suffering are some of the traits He is trying to develop in you while He works on and through you. He uses these challenges to build our character. So, regardless of the circumstances in which you find yourself, God is using them to get you where you need to be.

Don't give up! It is certain that if you give up, you will NEVER reach your destination. If you do give up, then what's next? What are you going to do? Die? If you don't die, you will have to start all over again from the beginning, and that is a waste of time no matter how you look at it. You will still face frustrations when you pursue goals and purpose, and all hell may break loose trying to stop you. So, have a made-up mind not to stop. Pick yourself up, brush yourself off, and continue moving. As long as you and I are alive, everyone suffers and goes through something. But each individual doesn't go through the exact same thing; they go through them at different times. It may be very similar, but we all face different situations and circumstances.

One may go through financial distress, while another faces sickness and disease, another experiences marital troubles, and yet another struggles with family issues. That is how life is. Although things change, a person will resolve one area of their life's problems, and something else will come up again. This is life's process.

It says in 1 Peter 5:10, "After you have suffered a while, He (God) will settle you, perfect you, establish and strengthen you." So, with this well-said verse, I do believe there is an expected and positive ending to all of this long-suffering as long as you and I follow through and don't give up.

Your Pain Is For A Greater Good

IT'S NOT ALL ABOUT YOU! Healing comes when you help others through their pain while you are going through yours. The reason for this is that your mind will no longer be preoccupied with focusing on yourself—me, myself, and I—or your own situation and pain. Instead, your focus will shift, and you will feel happy and uplifted knowing you are helping someone else with their problems. You will also feel much better realizing that you are not the only person facing challenges. This will help time pass more quickly, and before you know it, you are healed and have moved past your own difficulties.

In hindsight, when you look back, you will probably wonder why you were so upset and realize it was not worth your stress. Sometimes, we need to be led to situations that would not normally be part of our routine to volunteer and help others. You are not defined by your past experiences and pain. These experiences allow you to gain greater insight into your future. If you evaluate these experiences, whether good or bad, and use them to improve yourself by moving toward positive changes, you will benefit greatly.

The greater good will not only help you, but it will also help the next relationships and other people that may find themselves in similar situations and circumstances you have been through in your past.

Trusting The Process

Going through the process is very painful, as I have repeatedly stated. However, each person goes through it differently, and it ultimately leads to a better future.

We must have faith and trust the process, even though it is hard. God would not allow you and me to endure all this for nothing! It's for a reason and a season. It is to birth your future destiny. One cannot go through the fire without being tried and come out as pure gold. A diamond cannot become a diamond without going through darkness and pressure to emerge as beautiful as it is. If it is not processed through time and pressure, it would not become such a brilliant and magnificent stone.

The process will likely bring pain, loneliness, humiliation, shame, poverty, lack, barrenness, and failures to some people. Sometimes, because of what you are going through, even your own family will look down on you and turn away from you because they are ashamed of you as you go through your process.

Some think they are better than you because of material things! Others will point their finger and judge you, saying you are going through suffering and struggles because you are doing something wrong or have sinned in your life, while they don't understand or know that it's your process in order to become the person God wants you to be. Each individual's process is exclusively different! Some are longer than others. The quicker one submits, the faster one can pass the test and move to the next level.

Just as gold is refined by fire, so are you being refined by the processes of life's trials to build the inner man. Integrity is built through suffering. Major spiritual attacks from the enemy, persecution by people the enemy uses, afflictions, tribulations, storms, strife, homelessness, and hopelessness are all part of this refining process. It's not always the devil doing; sometimes when you are going through, it's God's doing for you to become pure gold. The surmounted fire and trials you face depend on what you are carrying, the anointing on your life. Don't be ashamed! You won't be here for long. When you are being persecuted, laugh at them in your heart and walk away if you must. So, in turn, when these are completed.

You and I must go through the same or similar pressure, isolation, and darkness to become the person God wants us to be. Your past pain has prepared you to be a better version of yourself! As long as you don't resist the process, when people see you, they won't see scars from your past. They will see only perfection. They won't see victims; they will see victors. They won't see abandoned; they will see claimed by the blood, continued, and moving forward. They will not see cursed but blessed. They won't see failure but fulfillment.

They won't see weaknesses but strengths, because of your past pain. So, I say to you, don't let your actions become the cause of someone else's stumbling block or pain. Be strong, powerful, and bold. People won't see rejection but acceptance. No more shame, humiliation, depression, oppression, torment, trials, hurt, and pain! No more Egypt, no more bondage! But victorious warriors.

No matter what adversity comes, one must stay goal-focused, because distractions will come to throw you off purpose. So, stay focused and go through the process. One cannot be used by the Lord unless they go through this process; one must be refined and processed before He can use them. The process takes time.

The purpose of processing is to build your character; it is formed only by going through the process. Going through the process will make you humble; it will take away behaviors that are not pleasing to God if you are not fighting against them with the flesh. The process will refine you and bring you to a level of faith, trust, confidence, and hope in God.

Going through the process will make you strong in God; the processing occurs in various stages that you must go through and pass the test. This is because of where you are going! God will remove some people who do not belong in your life and circle, or else they will hold you back. Where you are going, they cannot handle it. So, they become a hindrance to your progress, and He eventually removes them from your life.

When you come out of your Egypt, out of the bondage, remember who brought you out. When you are enjoying the good things in life—material things, nice homes, nice cars, financial prosperity, good food, good health—remember your God and seek His face and do His will. You and I cannot be stopped; our lives have been mapped out since the beginning of time, before we were born, even before our parents' substances were knit together, before God called our names before the existence of time. Our path may be slowed down by the enemy or circumstances, but it cannot be stopped! It may be diverted from the straight and narrow path to the curvy roads to get to our destination. But we cannot be stopped until we finish our course.

The End

Made in the USA
Columbia, SC
07 November 2024

45946362R00035